I0437346

FLAWED JUSTICE

WHEN OUR UNALIENABLE RIGHTS ARE IGNORED

BY

GEORGE E. PFAUTSCH

authorHOUSE®

AuthorHouse™
1663 Liberty Drive, Suite 200
Bloomington, IN 47403
www.authorhouse.com
Phone: 1-800-839-8640

© *2007 George E. Pfautsch. All rights reserved.*

*No part of this book may be reproduced, stored in
a retrieval system, or transmitted by any means
without the written permission of the author.*

First published by AuthorHouse 6/12/2007

ISBN: 978-1-4343-0960-0 (sc)

Library of Congress Control Number: 2007903492

Printed in the United States of America
Bloomington, Indiana

This book is printed on acid-free paper.

ACKNOWLEDGEMENTS AND THANKS

Considerable information for this book was obtained from the websites maintained by the United States Supreme Court Historical Society and by the White House. Additional information was obtained from the opinions in the cases reviewed and the United States Information Agency. Visits to The National Monument To The Forefathers in Plymouth, Massachusetts and to the United States Supreme Court provided insights and inspiration.

Thanks again to my wife, Dodi, for her patience and to Mary Lu for her editing and technical assistance.

Contents

INTRODUCTION

We make frequent references to justice, but justice is difficult to define. It is and has been defined in many ways and has different meanings to many of us. References are made to economic justice, social justice, legal justice, justice for the poor and other forms of justice. Justice is based on one's own concept of fairness, virtue and morality.

Justice and morality are closely related. Justice in the absence of morality is diminished and morality in the absence of justice is diminished. In the absence of faith both are diminished. However, views of faith are also almost as varied as are the views of justice.

"Life is not fair" is a common and true expression. Fairness is one way to define justice and therefore we must accept that justice too is not perfect.

Citizens of this country have been and continue to be blessed simply because they have been born in the greatest nation on earth. From that birthright, they have a decided advantage compared with someone born in a third world country. That to some degree is a social injustice. In the absence of a perfect universal governing body such injustices are impossible to overcome.

No matter how much governments, religions and others attempt to correct such injustices, they will never totally succeed. Such inequities have been in existence since the beginning of time and will remain in existence until the end of time. It is a laudable but impossible effort to eliminate that "injustice". It is also impossible because the definition of social justice varies substantially, and those in power have much to do with the determination of what is or is not just.

In this book, we will focus primarily on our legal justice system. It too will never be perfect but a more perfect system should be the never-ending goal.

In his farewell address to the nation on September 17, 1796, President George Washington stated, "virtue and morality must be the springboard to popular government". That statement can be extended to our justice system, which is a part of our government, because our legal justice system should not exist in a moral vacuum.

Despite a legal system, it was not possible for Jewish people to achieve justice in Germany during the Nazi regime. Hitler's immoral view of the Jewish race made that impossible.

LEGAL JUSTICE MUST HAVE A FIRM MORAL FOUNDATION ON WHICH IT IS BASED.

In his aforementioned farewell address to the nation, President Washington also stated the following: "Reason and experience forbid us to expect that national morality can prevail in exclusion of religious principle". What did President Washington mean?

In this book we will examine those instances when our national morality was ignored by our justice system and how such moral ignorance failed many in this country. We will also examine the reasons behind such failings.

President Washington's comment on "reason and experience" was true in 1796 and is also true more than 200 years later. Justice without a national morality is flawed and a national morality without some religious principles is also flawed. We will refer to that morality as our national faith-based morality.

CHAPTER 1 --- THE
BASICS OF JUSTICE

On a hill near the area where the Pilgrims landed in Plymouth, Massachusetts stands a monument dedicated to this country's forefathers. *THE NATIONAL MONUMENT TO THE FOREFATHERS* at 81 feet tall is an imposing sight. On the top of that monument is the central figure of FAITH, which alone stands 36 feet tall.

Below the central figure of FAITH are four figures symbolizing MORALITY, EDUCATION, LAW AND LIBERTY. The four symbols are meant to represent "the principles upon which the Pilgrim Fathers proposed to found their Commonwealth." Every tourist, who visits that monument, is provided with a considerable amount of symbolism to ponder.

As one contemplates the meaning, there should be no mistaking the interrelationship of the symbols. Above MORALITY, EDUCATION, LAW AND LIBERTY there is FAITH. When viewing the monument one is left to wonder how much value is detracted from the four sub-symbols if there is no faith above for guidance.

On the monument, LAW is portrayed as a draped male. His chair is supported by Justice (a woman with scales and sword) and Mercy. The symbols imply that LAW must be derived from FAITH as does MORALITY, EDUCATION AND LIBERTY. Then and only then can justice truly exist. That is not only symbolism, but also truth. That truth extends to the degree of justice present in a nation. Just law must incorporate faith. To have just laws, it is necessary to understand that the most basic of all rights; life, liberty and the pursuit of happiness are unalienable rights and are bestowed on us by our Creator. That belief, which was expressed by our founding fathers in the Declaration of Independence, requires faith.

Many countries have had laws that lacked justice. Nazi Germany and Fascist Italy had laws but lacked justice. Iraq under Saddam Hussein had laws but lacked justice. Communist Russia under Stalin had laws but lacked justice. When the founding fathers of this country declared their independence and created a Constitution, they incorporated the ingredients for justice portrayed on the monument in Plymouth. Subsequently, this country has been blessed with the best justice system the world has known.

The justice system of this country has a great history and much has been written and can still be written about the benefits this country has derived from it. However, in this book we will look at the times when the justice system has failed the citizens of this country. Those occurrences have generally taken place when the symbolism portrayed by *THE NATIONAL MONUMENT TO THE FOREFATHERS* has been ignored. When the principles incorporated into that monument, especially faith and morality are ignored, justice cannot be assured and sometimes that has been the case in this country's history.

Our founding fathers established the ingredients for justice when they signed the *DECLARATION OF INDEPENDENCE* and wrote the Preamble to our *CONSTITUTION.*

Included in the *DECLARATION OF INDEPENDENCE* are the words, "We hold these truths to be self-evident, that all men are created equal, that they are endowed by their Creator with certain unalienable rights, that among these are life, liberty and the pursuit of happiness". Those words were the primary reason that our founding fathers believed a new nation with those principles deserved to be created. Those words also embraced the principles of that monument in Plymouth. Those words also incorporate faith and morality as necessary values in the intended freedom for all citizens and in the justice such citizens deserved and were endowed with by their Creator.

In the Preamble to our *CONSTITUTION*, the founding fathers used the words, "We the people of the United States, in order to form a more perfect Union, establish Justice, insure domestic Tranquility, provide for the common defense, promote the general Welfare, and secure the Blessings of Liberty to ourselves and our Posterity, do ordain and establish the Constitution for the United States of America".

The above words from the *DECLARATION OF INDEPENDENCE* and the Preamble to the *CONSTITUTION* included the necessary language for establishing a just *CONSTITUTION* and just laws. It would be left to future individuals to see that the justice assumed in those words would be perpetually extended to the citizens of this nation.

The first ten amendments to the Constitution (the Bill of Rights) were ratified by our founding fathers on December 15, 1791. With those additions to the Constitution, the justice system of this country was founded on the basis of faith and morality. In the Declaration of Independence, faith was acknowledged by the declaration that certain unalienable rights were derived from the goodness of our Creator. In the Preamble, recognition was given to the need to promote the general welfare, and in the Bill of Rights the individual rights of citizens were set forth. The founding fathers did an excellent job of incorporating the symbols contained in the Monument to our Forefathers.

Even though the proper words were included in the documents founding this nation, it had to be left to future judges and jurists to carry out the justice intended in those documents. By and large the judges over the years have done a marvelous job of extending justice to the citizens of this country. But people including judges are fallible and in their fallibility we have had situations when justice was lacking. When justice was lacking, faith and faith-based morality too were lacking.

Even with the appropriate language in our founding documents, there were shortcomings in justice from the very beginning of this nation. Slavery was accepted in the southern colonies before the formation of this nation and then continued for another eighty-five plus years before it was abolished. It was one of the greatest injustices permitted in this country.

Justice was also lacking in the treatment of Native Americans. Many would be killed due to the early settlers desire for land, and the willingness of our government to treat them as less than citizens. Slavery also included Native Americans.

Women also were not treated as equal in this new country. They would have to wait almost 150 years before obtaining the right to vote.

At the present time the unborn of this nation are denied the unalienable right to life extended to them by our Creator. Parsing the words of the Constitution or laws should not and do not extend justice to the unborn. They remain unprotected in this society. The right to privacy should never be regarded as a higher right than the unalienable right to life. Humans extend to others the right of privacy but the unalienable right to life comes from our Creator. The founding fathers understood that, but today too many judges and politicians do not.

The injustices to African Americans, Native Americans and women were permitted to last far too long. Government and especially our judicial system did too little for too many years before correcting all but the last of the aforementioned injustices. The right to life remains to be extended to the unborn. It is an unalienable right but no longer viewed as such by our justice system.

Government could have and should have looked at the three basic premises our forefathers had written into the Declaration and Constitution and asked themselves three questions:

1 - In our treatment of slaves, Native Americans and women were we observing the belief that it was a self-evident truth that all men are created equal and endowed by their Creator with certain unalienable rights?

2 - In our treatment of slaves, Native Americans and women were we promoting the general welfare of all citizens and those who deserved to be citizens?

3 - In our treatment of slaves, Native Americans and women were we extending the Bill of Rights to all citizens or were we being selective as to who received the protection of those rights.

At this time in our history we should also be asking another question. In our treatment of the unborn, do we continue to ignore the justice our forefathers foresaw when declaring this nation's independence? If not, how many more years will government continue to support this basic injustice of denial to the unalienable right to life?

We will never be a perfect nation. We have been at times a great nation and at times a good nation, but we have had flaws in our government and especially in our judicial system. Those flaws can be reduced when we abide by the national faith-based morality intended by our founding fathers.

Our national faith-based morality requires government and citizens to understand that we receive certain unalienable rights from our Creator. It further requires government and all citizens to treat other citizens as they wish to be treated. Kindness to our fellow humans and a strong desire for freedom for all are the trademarks of faith-based morality. Government and, in particular, the judicial system of this country go awry when our national faith-based morality is not observed. Secular-based morality alone may not and often does not provide optimal justice for all.

Occasionally, all citizens and certainly all judges would be well served to take a trip to Plymouth, Massachusetts and ponder the symbols of *THE NATIONAL MONUMENT TO THE FOREFATHERS.* A reading of the first two sentences of the Declaration of Independence should be required before any judge renders a verdict. Every lawyer in this country should have to explain the intent of our forefathers' use of the words "self-evident truths" and "unalienable rights" before passing the bar. We sometimes lack justice because we ignore the basic ingredients of justice. Recognition of the fact that the Constitution is a secular document, which must be adjudicated with a basic understanding of our national faith-based morality seems to be forgotten by many judges today.

In this book we will examine some of the major shortcomings in the application of justice during the history of this country and why those shortcomings occurred. It would be wrong to imply that most of our shortcomings occurred at the early stages of this nation.

We have had and continue to have flaws in our justice system. The focus of this book will be the Supreme Court but will also include some lower courts and other branches of government, when their decisions have been at odds with moral justice.

When evaluating decisions made by the Supreme Court regarding Constitutional rights or wrongs we will most frequently go directly to the words of the Constitution. In that manner we can best compare such decisions to the intent of the founding fathers. Stare decisis (legal precedence) is fine but it has limitations and too often has been used as an excuse to extend injustices. Too often, decisions establishing legal precedence have eroded the original intent of the Constitution and have had a cascading effect on adding different intent than originally perceived. None of us can ever be absolutely certain of the original intent but using the language actually contained in the Constitution is as close as we can probably come.

CHAPTER 2 --- MARBURY VS. MADISON

Article III of the Constitution sets forth the judicial powers of the United States. Section 1 of Article III states that such power be vested in one Supreme Court and in such inferior courts as Congress deems necessary. In Section 2, the Constitution sets forth the "Cases" in which the Judiciary branch of government shall have jurisdiction. Those powers and duties were stated somewhat vaguely and it was left to Congress to further determine how far such jurisdiction would extend.

In 1789, Congress passed the Judiciary Act whereby they designated the federal circuit and district courts and provided that the Supreme Court include a Chief

Justice and five Associate Justices. The Supreme Court was the only court of appeal to the circuit and district courts.

The Supreme Court was required to meet twice a year. It did so but in its first few years it heard very few cases. We were a new nation with a new judicial system and therefore, very few cases at first moved to the Supreme Court.

In its first few years the Court also had to struggle with the degree of jurisdiction it believed it had, and with the vague description in the Constitution much of its subsequent powers would depend on its own precedence. It may be a flaw that the highest court of this land effectively has the power it believes it has. Such power can ignore the will of the people as well as the will of legislators, and is therefore akin to dictatorial power. When power is unrestrained and self-appointed it is only as good as those administering justice. Justices at the federal level are not elected and therefore not subject to removal by a democratic process. We shall examine instances where the failure to judge with the recognition of our national faith-based morality resulted in flawed and failed justice.

President Washington appointed John Jay the first Chief Justice of the Supreme Court. John Rutledge and Oliver Ellsworth followed him. The latter served as Chief Justice until 1800.

In the early years the Supreme Court's duties were less than glamorous. Congress initially required the judges to sit with the circuit courts and to do so twice a year. In 1793, that requirement was changed to once a year. Given the mode of travel at that time and the fact they also had to sit in session twice a year caused the early judges to spend a substantial amount of time traveling.

In late 1800, Chief Justice Ellsworth was ill and decided to resign. President John Adams appointed his Secretary of State, John Marshall to the Supreme Court and as Chief Justice. Adams would state "My gift of John Marshall to the people of the United States was the proudest act of my life". John Marshall would serve on the bench until his death in 1835. He would leave an imprint on the justice system and preside over a case that would be and still is studied in the law schools of this nation.

As John Adams was leaving office, politics played a significant role in our justice system. Thomas Jefferson, a Republican, succeeded Adams, a Federalist, in office. Before leaving office Adams and Congress took actions, which were intended to maintain Federalist ideals in the judicial system.

During the period following Adams' defeat at the hands of Jefferson, the lame duck Federalists in Congress enacted legislation reducing the Supreme Court membership to five thereby eliminating by one the number of justices that could be appointed and approved in the Jefferson administration. The new law also set up new circuit courts with sixteen new justices. As one of his final acts Adams appointed a number of judges to fill the new vacancies. Congress hastily approved the appointments and sent them at the last minute back to Adams to sign their commissions and they were then rushed to the State Department to affix the seal of the United States. This was to be done by John Marshall, who was still the Secretary of State, before he assumed his role as Chief Justice.

Politics had entered the selection and appointment of federal judges. Adams and the Federalists were attempting to pack the courts with judges sympathetic to Federalist causes. Soon after Jefferson was inaugurated, the new Congress repealed the last minute Judiciary Act the Federalists had enacted. The last minute enactment of the Judiciary Act by the Federalists, the appointment of "midnight judges" by Adams, and the repealing of the Judiciary Act by the Republicans were as political or more so than federal judicial appointments of current times. Politics and power go together and both require the checks and balances envisioned by the founding fathers.

During the process of trying to appoint the midnight judges, some of the commissions failed to be delivered. One of those failing to be delivered was for William Marbury of Washington, who had been appointed Justice of the Peace for the District of Columbia.

In December 1801, Marbury applied directly to the Supreme Court for his commission. He did this by requesting a "writ of mandamus" from the Court ordering James Madison to deliver the commission. By December 1801, Madison was the Secretary of State under Jefferson. In a surprise to many the Court agreed to hear the case.

The decision in Marbury vs. Madison was delivered in February 1803. Chief Justice Marshall wrote the opinion that Marbury did have a right to his commission and that the writ of mandamus he requested would enforce such a right. The important part of the decision was that the Court could not deliver that right.

The decision was of less importance than the principle the Court established. In the Judiciary Act of 1789, Congress said that the Court did have the constitutional jurisdiction in such a case. Marshall and the Court however said that the jurisdiction of the Court was established in the Constitution and Congress could not change it by the enactment of a law and that therefore that section of the law was void. Marshall proudly proclaimed "It is emphatically, the province and duty of the judicial department, to say what the law is." In the Marbury vs. Madison decision, the Supreme Court effectively decided that it had the sole power to interpret the Constitution and that remains a precedent to this day. Such power went beyond the powers set forth in Article III of the Constitution.

Let us assume for a minute that the Supreme Court had decided that it did not have the power to determine the constitutionality of laws enacted by Congress. In the case they heard Marbury would have been permitted to become the Justice of the Peace for Washington as intended by President Adams and the Congress prior to them leaving office. Would that have been a grave miscarriage of justice? No, and it would leave Congress and the President with the power to enact laws without interference from the Supreme Court. That may have been a better decision inasmuch as it would have better preserved the checks and balances of government.

There is no doubt that the decision put an inordinate amount of power in the hands of the Supreme Court as well as other courts. But was it a decision, which maintained the proper checks and balances of government, and did it improve justice for the citizens of this nation?

In this nation, the people elect the president and congress. Members of the Supreme Court are not elected. If the branch of government with the greatest amount of power is not elected by the people, is it a country of the people, by the people and for the people? Because the people elect the president and congress, it would seem that the greatest amount of power, in the matter of legislation, should rest with those two branches of government. In that manner, if for any reason the people feel that actions of the president and congress are not in their best interest, they can vote to remove them from office.

When the Supreme Court justices or other appointed justices do not act in the interest of the people they cannot be removed from office by the people, as can the president and congress. But in Marbury vs. Madison a certain amount of power was transferred from the president and congress to the judicial system. In effect, it also transferred power away from the people, because the members of the judiciary are not directly accountable to the people. Therefore, Marbury vs. Madison set a dangerous precedent. It permitted the only body of government not elected by the people to trump the decisions of the two bodies of government that are elected.

Legal scholars can properly argue that Marbury vs. Madison clarified the authority of the Supreme Court. However, that argument has nothing to do with a system that should provide the greatest justice for all citizens of a country. If the judicial system can trump the decisions of the president and of congress, then effectively it can also trump the will of the people. Marbury vs. Madison, by increasing the power of those not elected by the people, diminished the role of the electorate and in doing so also diminished the role of democracy for this nation. If the members of the Supreme Court can thumb their noses at the will of the people and make decisions that are not in accord with the will of the people, then the opportunity for abuse of power exists just as it does for those governed in other nations by dictators. In effect the judicial system has dictatorial powers.

Marbury vs. Madison gave the appointed judicial officials of this country the opportunity to effectively say, "It is our Constitution and not the Constitution of the people because we can decide what it means and it matters not if the president, congress or the people don't agree".

If Marbury vs. Madison did give excessive power to the Court then those of us who believe that, have an obligation to propose a system that would permit the Court to rule on constitutional matters within a framework that better aided a government of the people, by the people and for the people.

In a democracy, should the Court be the final arbiter of the intent of the Constitution? The answer to that is yes, as regards cases other than those deciding the constitutionality of laws passed by Congress.

Should the Supreme Court be the final arbiter as to whether or not laws passed by the legislative branch of government meet the intent of the Constitution? That is a far more difficult answer in a democracy wherein legislators are elected and the judges are not. Considering that many members of Congress are members of the legal profession and that there are 535 ELECTED members, it seems that a democracy might be as well or better served if the members of Congress are the final enactors and decision makers as to what laws meet the requirements of the Constitution. If they take action that is contrary to the will of the people then they can be removed by the votes of the people. A Constitutional Amendment would be the best method of letting the people make that decision. We need to remember that it was the Supreme Court at the time of Marbury vs. Madison and not Congress that decided it had the power to decide the constitutionality of laws passed by Congress.

What would such a Constitutional Amendment state? It should state that the Supreme Court is not the final arbiter of the constitutionality of laws passed by Congress and signed into law by the President. It would be appropriate for the Supreme Court to refer laws back to Congress when it believed laws passed by Congress violated some aspect of the Constitution. It would then be the duty of Congress to correct such violations IF CONGRESS believed it necessary to do so.

It may well be that under the constitutional powers granted to Congress, they could pass a law stating they were the final arbiters of the intent of laws they enacted as to whether or not such laws were constitutional. However, with 200 years of precedent to the contrary, it would be better to have a Constitutional Amendment that makes that clarification. It would also preclude a potentially harmful power struggle between the legislative and judicial branches of our government.

It is a risky proposition in a democracy to have non-elected judges determine the degree of power they possess in determining not only the intent of the Constitution, but also if laws enacted by elected federal officials are constitutional. This author does not like all laws enacted but it would be a greater comfort to this citizen to know that my elected officials are the final arbiters of laws that meet a constitutional standard. It is far more difficult to believe that nine non-elected judges of a Supreme Court will better serve a government of the people, by the people and for the people.

The rest of this book will be devoted to covering those situations when our current judicial system failed to deliver justice. Far too frequently, power in the hands of the non-elected members of our judicial system has been abused in determining justice for citizens without any recourse or retribution by the citizens. Federal judges do possess certain dictatorial powers under our current system of government.

CHAPTER 3 --- THE MALIGNED FIRST AMENDMENT

WE ASK THAT ALL CITIZENS OF THIS NATION BE THANKFUL FOR THE UNALIENABLE RIGHTS OF LIFE, LIBERTY AND THE PURSUIT OF HAPPINESS ENDOWED UPON THEM BY YOU, OUR CREATOR. FOR THESE RIGHTS WE ARE THANKFUL.

WE ASK THAT THROUGH OUR FAITH IN YOU, AS SYMBOLIZED IN A MONUMENT TO OUR FOREFATHERS, WE ALWAYS BE GUIDED PROPERLY IN MATTERS OF MORALITY, EDUCATION, LAW AND LIBERTY.

WE ASK YOU, OUR CREATOR, THAT OUR ULTIMATE PURVEYORS OF JUSTICE, THE MEMBERS OF OUR SUPREME COURT, SEEK THE WISDOM PORTRAYED IN THE SYMBOLS OF JUSTICE WHICH ADORN THE BUILDING AND ESPECIALLY THE ROOM IN WHICH THEY PRESIDE.

IN GOD WE TRUST.

Are the above words prayers? Would they be permitted to be said every morning in a public school? Have we betrayed the intent of the First Amendment by even having to ask the question? Have we reached the ridiculous stage, where the words in our own Declaration of Independence may constitute a religious prayer and not be eligible for display in public places?

As you probably have guessed the above words come from words in our Declaration of Independence, from words on our currency, from reflections on the symbols of a monument in Plymouth, Massachusetts, and from reflections on the symbols on and in the Supreme Court of this country. Who knows? By the strange logic of some Supreme Court members maybe the display of the Ten Commandments on our Supreme Court building is a violation of the Establishment Clause of the First Amendment. Have we reached the stage in this country where we believe the forefathers made a statement of faith in the Declaration of Independence and then contradicted it in the First Amendment? It seems positively, absolutely, and unequivocally clear that the forefathers believed faith, virtue, or national morality did not have the same meaning as religion.

In the past fifty years the highest court of this country has had great difficulty in differentiating between faith and religion. Faith is the belief in something, including a Creator and unalienable rights that cannot be proven. A person can have faith in God without being religious or belonging to any religion (faith-based morality). Religion is a specific set of beliefs and practices encompassing a group of people who agree on such practices and beliefs (religion-based morality) and form an institution for the purpose of practicing such beliefs.

THE SUPREME COURT HAS TOTALLY BLURRED THE DISTINCTION BETWEEN FAITH AND RELIGION. Most of that blurring has occurred in the past fifty years and is probably due to the Supreme Court's slow but steady shift to judgments based on a secular morality despite the intent of our founding fathers. In doing so the Court ignores the words in our Declaration of Independence and in the Preamble to the Constitution.

In the early 1960's, the New York State Board of Regents prepared a "non-denominational" prayer for use in the public schools. The words of the prayer were

"Almighty God, we acknowledge our dependence upon Thee, and we beg Thy Blessing upon us, our parents, our teachers and our Country".

In one school district a group of parents challenged the prayer as being "contrary to the beliefs, religions, or religious practices of both themselves and their children". The Supreme Court of New York ruled in favor of the state because the state did not force any student to join in the prayer if a parent objected. That seemed to be a wise and proper ruling. Whose right is being violated if one is not forced to participate in a "non-denominational prayer" that had no specific relationship to any religion?

The Supreme Court of the United States came to a different conclusion. The highest court of this land believed that a state-sponsored prayer was contrary to the spirit and command of the First Amendment's ban against the establishment of religion. In the majority's decision, note was made that a prayer by any definition constituted a religious activity. That is more than a stretch. It is fallacious. PRAYER IS A COMMUNICATION WITH OUR CREATOR OR OTHER OBJECT OF WORSHIP. PRAYER MAY BE A RELIGIOUS ACTIVITY BUT IS NOT NECESSARILY A RELIGIOUS ACTIVITY.

Prayer is possible for someone who is not involved in any religion. It is an activity available to every person on earth even if they have never been exposed to any religion. Is reciting a portion of the Declaration of Independence a religious activity? It states this country's belief that a Creator endows the unalienable rights. Did the words at the beginning of this chapter constitute a prayer? Was not our country founded on the belief of those words? Should they be banned from recitation in public schools? New York's highest court was correct in its view that as long as a prayer was not required to be recited, it did not violate anything. In fact, part of the First Amendment regarding free speech authorizes non-denominational prayer. In a flawed attempt to link a non-denominational prayer to the establishment clause the Court violated the prohibition clause of the First Amendment. PRAYER CAN BE AN ACITIVITY OF FAITH WITHOUT BEING A "RELIGIOUS ACTIVITY". When government denies expressions of faith as opposed to expresses of religion, it violates the First Amendment. Faith and religion ARE NOT words that have the same meaning and the founding fathers did not intend them to have the same meaning when interpreting the First Amendment.

The First Amendment states that "Congress shall make no law respecting an establishment of religion, or prohibiting the free exercise thereof". What did our founding fathers have in mind? Might it not have been the simple belief that Congress should not establish the Anglican, Catholic or other specific religion as the "official" church of state as had been done in countries of Europe. Given the situation at that period of time, there is more logic in that reasoning than there is in the reasoning made by too many judges in modern times regarding non-religious activities.

In my book "Redefining Morality - A Threat to our Nation", I gave numerous examples indicating that we have drifted toward a secular morality in this country and thereby threaten the society envisioned by our forefathers. When morality becomes secular there is no adherence to the belief in the unalienable rights endowed on us by our Creator. One of the major forces in this country moving us more and more toward a secular morality is the judicial system of this country. It has twisted the "establishment clause" to a degree that would make it difficult for the founding fathers to recognize their reason for that clause. They were brilliant in there view that Congress should make no law respecting an establishment of religion. Congress has fulfilled its requirement far better than the Supreme Court has in interpreting that requirement. The Court has taken a much more intrusive role in self-interpreting the establishment clause than it has in being concerned about prohibiting the free exercise of religion. In the name of the establishment clause it tramples on the prohibition clause and on the freedom of speech, which is also part of the First Amendment.

Let us look at some other convolutions of justice as regards the establishment clause.

In 1980 the Supreme Court, in Stone vs. Graham, held that a Kentucky statute requiring the posting of a copy of the Ten Commandments on a wall of each public school was unconstitutional, inasmuch as it did not serve a secular legislative purpose, and therefore violated the Establishment Clause of the First Amendment. Someone should have told them that serving a "secular legislative purpose" is not the only requirement of justice. In fact, someone should have reminded them of President Washington's comment on what it takes to have a national morality.

While the Kentucky legislature may have been excessively aggressive in its requirements, the Supreme Court was no better in its rationale for overturning the legislation. The Court stated that the pre-eminent purpose for posting the Ten Commandments on schoolroom walls is plainly religious in nature. I wonder which religion they are discussing. The court said the Ten Commandments are a sacred text in the Jewish and Christian faiths. Which specific religion in the Jewish and Christian faiths were they talking about? They erred. The state of Kentucky's requirement did not violate the Establishment Clause that prohibits laws respecting establishment of religion. The display of the Ten Commandments is merely a display of faith in our Creator and some degree of faith was also recognized in our Declaration of Independence. Should we be forced to refute what is said in our Declaration of Independence? If so, why did we become a new nation in 1776?

As long as the Court keeps blurring the distinction between "religion" and "faith" they will continue to be oppressive in permitting people to express their right to exercise their freedom of speech in regards to faith. Unfortunately the Supreme Court ignores that part of the First Amendment as it stretches further and further in its pursuit of striking down symbols of faith, which are not the specific endorsement of any single religion.

In 1989, the Supreme Court ruled that a nativity scene in the Allegheny County Courthouse was not permissible under the Establishment Clause because it was a religious display. Two things were wrong with that decision. The establishment clause states that Congress shall make no law respecting an establishment of religion. In this case (Allegheny County v ACLU) no such law was involved and in reality the Supreme Court had no right to meddle because Congress had made no law. That was problem number one. Problem two was that the Supreme Court again was confusing religion and faith. The nativity scene is not claimed by any specific religion. Broad symbols of faith DO NOT VIOLATE the words of the Establishment Clause.

In the first two of the three cases cited in this chapter, state legislative officials were involved in establishing a requirement to be followed by schools. To that extent it was more understandable that the Courts would be involved at the highest level in adjudicating such mandates, even if their rationale in making their decisions were flawed.

The purpose in citing each of the above cases is to point out that the Supreme Court in the past fifty years has taken the view that if it is not secular it must be religious. That ignores the entire belief our forefathers had that this country would be best served by pursuing a national or faith-based morality. It would neither endorse a specific religion nor would it be a country that only viewed legislation from solely a secular perspective.

The members of the Supreme Court and other Courts no longer seem to understand what our first president so profoundly stated in his farewell address.

It is unfortunate that this country has very few advocates that fight for our national faith-based morality in pursuit of justice. It seems that the arguments of society as well as the courts have a warped perspective as relates to the first part of the First Amendment. If it's not secular it must be religious. That view is tearing our society apart. It is also causing injurious acrimony between our political parties and certainly is a serious definitional flaw of our judicial system.

On one hand, the Court is abusing the intent of the religious portion of the First Amendment in denying the rights of those who wish to maintain faith, faith-based symbols and faith-based morality in this country. On the other hand it has no qualms permitting almost anything that comes remotely close to denying the freedom of speech or the press, which is also a part of the First Amendment. They are too frequently oblivious to the Preamble of the Constitution, which states that we the people do ordain and establish this Constitution to promote the General Welfare among other things.

Pornography, explicit sexual pictures and displays, four-letter language on television and in the movies must somehow promote the general welfare because there is no limitation on the entertainment or news media in their use.

One is left to wonder why the religious aspects of the First Amendment are so tightly interpreted as to ban almost anything that relates to the faith of citizens in this country even if many do not belong to any religion, while at the same time permitting almost anything under the label of freedom of speech and the press.

It is hard to attribute such decisions to anything other than the pursuit of secular morality or diabolical reasoning and justice will not be served when the endower of all unalienable rights of life, liberty and pursuit of happiness is removed from the judicial equation. That is not a novel thought of this author. It is the reason this country was created by our founding fathers. As noted in the introduction of this book, justice is lacking when faith is lacking.

Some current and former members of the Supreme Court have recently expressed some dismay at the hostility shown the Court by members of Congress and of the public. They could spare themselves such dismay by interpreting the Constitution in accordance with the wishes of our forefathers instead of the politically correct and solely secular moral viewpoint prevailing at this current point in our history.

CHAPTER 4 --- SCOTT VS. SANFORD AND SLAVERY

Slavery was introduced to this country in the early seventeenth century. In 1619, a Dutch trader exchanged his cargo of Africans to settlers in Jamestown for food. It is not clear if the intent was for the Africans to become "indentured servants", as was the case with Europeans who were willing to be indentured for a number of years as laborers in exchange for the right of passage to this country.

In some areas the Africans were given their freedom after a period of years, but as tobacco became a highly profitable crop in Virginia and Maryland, the tobacco plantations became more and more dependent on these "servants". In the middle of the seventeenth century the idea of "perpetual servitude" or slavery became more entrenched in Virginia, Maryland and eventually other southern colonies.

In a country that had been founded on the belief that it was a "self-evident truth" that all people are created equal, slavery was an abomination and will forever be a stain on the history of this nation. Slaves were beaten and killed and were often separated from their family. For a period of time Native Americans also were forced into slavery, but it gradually became more prevalent among the natives of Africa.

Slavery eventually became a political and sectional issue in this country. By the middle of the nineteenth century more than 40,000 plantations in the south owned at least twenty slaves and more than half the slaves worked on these large plantations. Plantation owners had a huge economic interest in maintaining slavery and were politically powerful. They were supported in their desire to maintain slavery by smaller farmers who also owned slaves and by many poorer whites who feared slaves would compete for jobs and land if they were set free. With that large majority of people favoring slavery, businessmen as well as professional people and political leaders of the south also found it expedient to support slavery.

During the early and mid-nineteenth century, slavery became a national political issue. As this nation grew some states were being admitted as slave states while others were admitted as free states. It was a political issue in Congress and it was a political issue in presidential elections and during presidential administrations. It was an issue that would also find its way into the judicial system of this country.

John Emerson was a surgeon in the Army. In 1833, while living in St. Louis, Emerson acquired Dred Scott to be his personal slave. He subsequently moved to Illinois, which was a free state that did not recognize slavery. After Emerson's death, Scott and his wife in 1846 sued for their freedom because Scott had been taken to free states and Missouri followed the "once free always free" rule. After a Circuit Court initially ruled against Scott the case was permitted to be reheard and in 1850 a judge in the second case sided with Scott but that decision did not put a final ending to the case.

In 1852, Mrs. Emerson appealed to the Missouri Supreme Court and that Court overturned the Circuit Court decision and thereby returned Scott to slavery.

After her husband's death, Mrs. Emerson eventually remarried and left her affairs in Missouri in the hands of her brother, John Sanford. During 1853 and 1854, Scott supported by lawyers who opposed slavery, again filed for his freedom, but this time the suit was filed in the U.S. Federal Court in St. Louis. This court also ruled against Scott.

In 1856, lawyers appealed the Federal Court decision to the U.S. Supreme Court. In 1857, the Supreme Court ruled that as a slave, Scott was not a citizen of this country and therefore had no standing to file a case in federal court. Unfortunately, the Court went even further in its disgrace of moral justice. The majority of justices broadened the scope of their decision, when they discovered that the two justices who were going to dissent and state that Congress had the right to control the issue of slavery in territories and had done so in the Missouri Compromise. The minority view of the two judges would have meant that Scott was not a slave and was a citizen.

The dissenting judges opinion would have left open the issue if free slaves and free Africans were citizens. The majority in the opinion written by Chief Justice Taney ruled that no "Negro", even if free, could be a citizen of this country. And for only the second time ever, it ruled a law of Congress, the Missouri Compromise, to be unconstitutional.

That effectively meant that Scott as a slave remained "personal property" of his owner because the Court ruled that Congress could not forbid citizens from taking their property, (slaves) into any territory owned by the United States.

Despite all the moral injustices rendered upon Dred Scott by the Courts, he died a free man. Mrs. Emerson had married a man opposed to slavery and decided to return Scott to the Blow family from whom her first husband had acquired him. The Blows in turn gave Scott his freedom. Although freed, he would die in 1858 and was denied citizenship due to the ruling of the

Taney Court. A few years later the Civil War and the thirteenth and fourteenth amendments would correct the injustices rendered by the Courts in several of the Dred Scott decisions.

In order to better understand how seven justices, who concurred in the majority opinion of the Dred Scott decision, could come to such a distortion of justice, presented below are the first three paragraphs of the decision written by Chief Justice Taney. The three paragraphs relate to Scott's status as a citizen of the United States.

The question is simply this: Can a Negro, whose ancestors were imported into this country, and sold as slaves, become a member of the political community formed and brought into existence by the Constitution of the United States, and as such become entitled to the rights, and privileges, and immunities, guarantied by that instrument to the citizen? One of which rights is the privilege of suing in a court of the United States in the cases specified in the constitution...

The words "people of the United States" and "citizens" are synonymous terms, and mean the same thing. They both describe the political body who, according to our republican institutions, form the sovereignty, and who hold the power and conduct the government through their representatives. They are what we familiarly call the "sovereign people," and every citizen is one of this people, and a constituent member of this sovereignty. The question before us is, whether the class of persons described in the plea in abatement compose a portion of this people, and are constituent members of this sovereignty? We think they are not, and that they are not included, and were not intended to be included, under the word "citizens" in the constitution, and can therefore claim none of the rights and privileges, which that instrument provides for and secures to citizens of the United States. On the contrary, they were at the time considered as a subordinate and inferior class of beings, (author's note - what happened to the self-evident truth that all men are created equal) *who had been subjugated by the dominant race, and, whether emancipated or not, yet remained subject to their authority, and had no rights or privileges but such as those who held the power and the government might choose to grant them.*

It is not the province of the court to decide upon the justice or injustice, the policy or impolicy, of these laws. The decision of that question belonged to the political or lawmaking power: to those who formed the sovereignty and framed the constitution. The duty of the court is, to interpret the instrument they have framed, with the best lights we can obtain on the subject, and to administer it as we find it, according to its true intent and meaning when it was adopted.

In the second paragraph provided above the Court subjectively determined who did not qualify as a citizen and in the third paragraph they apologize for not being permitted to be subjective. It is a chilling and sober opinion that indicates what can happen when the final purveyors of justice in this country seek to ignore our national faith-based morality in their interpretations and decide to interpret in a purely secular matter, ignoring the basic rights endowed by our Creator. It was unfortunately not only a miscarriage of justice but also a willful miscarriage of justice with the attempt to blame the framers of the constitution with the miscarriage. It was sickening in its degree of injustice and it was sickening in their attempt to blame the framers of the constitution.

The Dred Scott vs. Sanford case should be a reminder to all of us that too much power at the highest level of government can be a danger to all citizens. Fortunately, for the slaves, three years after the Dred Scott case, we would have a president, Abraham Lincoln, who would effectively say, "This injustice cannot and will not be permitted to stay in place". He risked the unity of this country and fought the bloodiest war fought on this nation's soil to correct the injustice. No other president has had the courage to ignore an egregious decision of our Supreme Court. The Emancipation Proclamation did ignore the Scott vs. Sanford decision even if it was done by executive order in a manner that circumvented the terrible decision of the Court.

The Supreme Court's sad history regarding slavery did not end with the Dred Scott case.

In 1873, in what is referred to as the Slaughterhouse cases the Supreme Court concluded that no new privileges or immunities were contained in the Fourteenth Amendment to protect African Americans from state power. It is very difficult to read Section 1 of the Fourteenth Amendment and come to that conclusion. It states that *No State shall make or enforce any law which shall abridge the privileges or immunities of citizens of the United States; nor shall any State deprive any person of life, liberty, or property, without due process of law: nor deny to any person within its jurisdiction the equal protection of the laws.*

It is difficult at the present time in history to believe that the duty of faith-based morality to love our neighbor and show kindness to others extended to members of the Supreme Court in the aforementioned decisions. Their rulings managed to interpret the words of the Constitution in a racist manner. Despite the efforts of President Lincoln, the thousands of men who lost their lives fighting the Civil War, and those in Congress and citizens who managed to add Amendments to the Constitution to protect African Americans, it appeared that a few Supreme Court Justices who should have been in the forefront of ensuring liberty for black American were doing the opposite.

The Court's sad history regarding African Americans continued in 1896. In a case decided that year, Plessy vs. Ferguson, the Court gave legal status to desegregation. In the south, following the Civil War, most states passed "Jim Crow laws" that created "separate but equal" facilities. The word equal was a stretch in many if not most or all situations. The practice of having separate facilities for African Americans covered most aspects of life in the South. The Plessy vs. Ferguson case was brought to the courts to decide if the Jim Crow laws were constitutional.

Homer Plessy agreed to be the test case for a group organized in New Orleans to challenge the Jim Crow laws of Louisiana. Plessy was a Creole who was one-eighth black, but under the Louisiana laws was classified as "colored". Plessy purchased a ticket on a train from New Orleans to Covington and was arrested for violation of the Louisiana law.

His lawyers argued that the laws violated both the thirteenth and fourteenth amendments of the Constitution, which had been passed after the Civil War. The Louisiana Courts upheld the constitutionality of the laws and the case went to the Supreme Court.

On May 18, 1896 the Supreme Court ruled that the thirteenth Amendment applied only to slavery and the separation of the races did not imply that one race was superior to the other. If the justices really believed that they must have been blind to the difference in quality of the separate but equal facilities. Unfortunately those in power have the ability to interpret words to meet the end results they wish to achieve. The Supreme Court did that in case after case relating to African Americans. The justice who wrote the opinion for the majority in the Plessy case added that the long-standing customs of society had to be taken into consideration. It again appeared that when the majority wished, the Court could be subjective in its interpretations.

The decision in the Plessy case was decided by a seven-to-one vote with one abstention. Justice John

Marshall Harlan cast the dissenting vote. His words of dissent were eloquent and bore greater moral justice on the issue of slavery and African Americans than had ever been uttered by the Court to that point in its history. His dissent included the following words:

...But in view of the Constitution, in the eye of the law, there is in this country no superior, dominant, ruling class of citizens. There is no caste here. Our Constitution is color-blind, and neither knows nor tolerates classes among citizens. In respect of civil rights, all citizens are equal before the law. The humblest is the peer of the most powerful. The law regards man as man, and takes no account of his surroundings or of his color when his civil rights as guaranteed by the supreme law of the land are involved. It is, therefore, to be regretted that this high tribunal, the final expositor of the fundamental law of the land, has reached the conclusion that it is competent for a State to regulate the enjoyment by citizens of their civil rights solely upon the basis of race.

In my opinion, the judgment this day rendered will, in time, prove to be quite as pernicious as the decision made by this tribunal in the Dred Scott case...The present decision, it may well be apprehended, will not only stimulate aggressions, more or less brutal and irritating, upon the admitted rights of colored citizens, but will encourage the belief that it is possible, by means of state enactments, to defeat the beneficent purposes which the people of the United States had in view when they adopted the recent amendments of the Constitution, by one of which the blacks of this country were made citizens of the United States and of the States in which they respectively reside, and whose privileges and immunities, as citizens, the States are forbidden to abridge...

Justice Harlan not only covered the constitutional requirements from a faith-based moral aspect but he was proven correct in his prognostications. In the Plessy case the Supreme Court of this country aided and abetted in the segregation of this country, which would continue for almost an additional sixty years. It had the opportunity to bring segregation to a halt but it failed to do so. It helped make a bad decision even worse and in that regard may have been more harmful than the Dred Scott decision.

Segregation would continue legally unchecked until 1956 when the decision in Brown vs. Board of Education dealt with several instances of segregation in public schools, and which declared segregation in schools to be unconstitutional. That decision was a harbinger of change, and subsequently the Civil Rights Act of 1964 and the Voting Rights Act of 1965 helped to finally undo what too many poorly adjudicated cases at the State and Federal Court levels had failed to do. In this and other instances Congress and the Executive branch did far more to bring justice to a class of people than did the judicial system, which should have that responsibility.

The excessive power granted to itself in Marbury vs. Madison, was a tool used by the Supreme Court to extend slavery and thereafter segregation. To this day the opportunity exists for the Supreme Court to make what amounts to dictatorial decisions. When it makes morally bankrupt decisions, it is difficult for Congress or the Executive Branch to redress the wrongs extended or created by the highest court of the land. Abraham Lincoln was a rare individual inasmuch as he refused to be bound by the injustice of the Dred Scott decision.

CHAPTER 5 --- ROE VS. WADE AND UNALIENABLE RIGHTS

In my previous books, "Redefining Morality" and "Times of Greatness", I dedicated a fairly large amount of space to the terrible wrongs of abortion. Nevertheless, it and other terminations of life deserve a chapter in this book as well because of the terrible injustice inherent in denying a human being the unalienable right to life.

One of the few defenses for abortions made by pro-choice advocates is that women should have the right to choose. Up to the point of conception I agree with that view. But once a woman is pregnant, the right to choose not only implies but also explicitly views the right to privacy as a greater right than the right to life. It may surprise readers but this author believes in the right to privacy. But that right should never be a greater right than the unalienable right to life.

From a national faith-based morality perspective, abortions must rank with slavery among the worst evils permitted in this country. Both violate the reasons our forefathers set forth in the Declaration of Independence to become a new country. In both situations judges and political leaders ignore the unalienable rights of life and liberty. All the other rights included in our Constitution must be subordinate to those unalienable rights. The rights set forth in our Constitution generally refer to the secular rights of citizens. But the rights set forth in the Declaration of Independence, as our forefathers stated, are endowed by our Creator and thus neither the judicial branch nor the legislative branch of government should ever be permitted to take away those rights. When government refuses to acknowledge through their actions that such rights are unalienable they inflict much harm to the value system of a society.

It is tremendously difficult to ever attempt to justify the devaluation of human life. In that regard abortions do parallel the injustices of slavery. I know that many readers will not agree that abortions rank with slavery in the denigration of moral justice. When I asked a good friend of mine, which was the more immoral of the two, his reply was that they were quite different. I agree with that but I do not draw any conclusions as to which is more evil in the eyes of our Creator. We became a country based on the belief that it is self-evident that the unalienable right to life is endowed by a Creator but we certainly fail to demonstrate that with our cavalier attitude toward life. If we truly believe that life is an unalienable right, then the ultimate judgment on the value of each and every human life is best left to our Creator.

In the Dred Scott case the justices of the Supreme Court rationalized that black American slaves did not belong to a class of people that deserved the status of "citizens". In Roe vs. Wade the justices again rationalized that unborn human beings did not deserve the status of "citizen" or "person". By parsing the English language, justices in both cases were able to rationalize that the unalienable rights of life and liberty did not extend to everyone.

In both cases the Supreme Court of this country departed from the self-evident truth that all people are created equal. That is the grave risk of secular-based morality. It has no foundation for basing decisions that result in the greatest degree of justice to all humanity.

To some people who believe in a religion-based morality the injustice of abortion may be as great or greater than slavery because of their belief in an immortal soul. No one can ever justify the horrors of slavery but in the belief of religion-based morality their souls after death may enjoy a greater happiness because of the suffering they endured on earth. The souls of unborn humans are not even given that opportunity. As noted earlier the judgment regarding the greater moral evil will be left to the judgment of our Creator as recognized by those with a religion-based morality.

As was the case with slavery, many in government are now defending the right to abortions. In the case of slavery many people in government rationalized the existence of slavery for political and economic reasoning and unfortunately the Supreme Court sided with those views. In the case of abortions, the Supreme Court again decided against the value of life and many politicians support that view.

In the case of slavery, that inhumane view of people was permitted to exist from a period prior to this nation's existence and for more than eighty years after it came into existence. It took an unusual and brave leader, Abraham Lincoln, to defy the decision of the Supreme Court and to make one of the greatest moral judgments in the history of human beings. In the case of abortions, we have now had more than thirty years of living with the Supreme Court's decision in Roe vs. Wade. If this country is ever again to wear the mantle of greatness that decision too will be overturned some day.

As long as the Supreme Court of this country has the dictatorial power to decide the constitutionality of laws it is extremely difficult for the people's wishes or for the other branches of government's wishes to prevail. The balance of power is distorted because the government of the people, by the people and for the people does not exist, when members of our federal judicial system decide they have the power to set aside laws or determine what the laws should be without any recourse by the other branches of government or by the people. When the Supreme Court makes a decision against the unalienable rights of life and liberty as they did in Scott vs. Sanford and again in Roe vs. Wade, they demonstrate the dictatorial powers they granted to themselves in Marbury vs. Madison.

It is now unfortunate that most of the members of the Democratic Party have aligned themselves with the Roe vs. Wade Supreme Court decision and with the lobbyists who also support that decision. Again there is a parallel with slavery. The support of slavery was from a section of the country. The support for abortions comes from most of the members of an entire political party.

Members of the Democratic Party in Congress never answer the following questions:

1. Is the right to privacy greater than the unalienable right to life?
2. Why does the unalienable right to life not extend to unborn human beings?
3. Is it relevant that many people believe in the existence of an immortal soul and that such existence begins at conception?

They cannot be put in the political position of answering those questions because if they answer any one of them they undermine their rationale for the permission to terminate the life of unborn human beings and future citizens of this nation. The members of the Supreme Court and the members of the Democratic Party in Congress cannot escape some of the blame for the more than 45 million abortions that have taken place in this country since the Roe vs. Wade decision.

In this book I do not want to review all the moral wrongs of abortion but rather to relate poor moral judgments made by our government especially our judicial system. If any reader wishes to look at additional reasons for the faith-based immorality related to abortions I refer them to Chapter 5 of my book, *REDEFINING MORALITY.*

It is not only through abortions that life is being devalued in the country. The state of Oregon now permits euthanasia. In other states this form of terminating human life is also under consideration. There seems to be less and less reasoning for people to believe that the unalienable right to life is the greatest right, we as human beings will ever have. When we have a better understanding of the value of life and its origin and the Creator of life, then we will have a better understanding that it is not in the province of humans to decide when another human being's life should be terminated.

Earlier I blamed the Democratic Party for helping to support the ongoing legal permissibility of abortions. To let the reader wonder to which political party I may be affiliated, let me now turn on the Republican Party. That party for too long has been the party that wishes to continue the death penalty as the ultimate form of capital punishment. It is wrong for any one group of humans to assume they have the right to determine who may live or not live. To take the life of another human being, no matter how severe his or her injustices to society may have been, is wrong. The ultimate vengeance for crimes is a matter that should be left to our Creator.

There is another reason that the death penalty should be outlawed. It is not necessarily the harshest form of punishment and therefore may not be any greater deterrent to reducing crime than other forms of punishment. I see nothing wrong with life imprisonment without the possibility of parole for those who commit the most heinous of crimes. It may be just as effective a deterrent as death and it may also be as severe a penalty. In addition it gives the offender the remainder of his life to redeem his offense.

Several readers of my earlier books have questioned me as to why I spend such little time on the morality issues related to war, because wars also result in the involuntary termination of life. Given that I write at length about the gift of life, that is a fair question. In my previous books I have indicated that this country is less inclined at this point in its history to be involved in wars that are fought to assure the freedom of citizens of other nations. One of the reasons I have not delved too deep into this area is my personal view that the moral justification for wars is tremendously difficult albeit at times morally justified.

Should we have been involved in the Revolutionary War, which resulted in the birth of this nation, and did the desire for freedom on a number of issues merit the loss of lives that were entailed in creating a new nation? That first war and many others we have been involved in as a nation are difficult to dissect from a moral standpoint. How much oppression of life, liberty and the pursuit of happiness justify a war?

It is my opinion that wars are justified when the freedom of others is substantially oppressed. At the same time it is my belief that the justification for any war be the very, very last resort to obtain the freedom for one's own citizens or for citizens of other nations. I view wars much as I view my own liberty or that of my family. At what point am I permitted to injure or even kill someone else to save my own life or that of a family member? Am I ever permitted to terminate another's life even if that person is a definite and very distinctive threat to my life or liberty? Must I wait until a gun is pointed at my head and it may be too late for defense? When I know the answer to those questions, I will feel more qualified to comment on the morality of wars. The justifications are always somewhat clouded.

From the inception of this universe to the present time we as flawed human beings have been involved in the waging of wars. When those wars are waged, as too many have been, to advance the power of a dictator or a nation, it is easy to find moral fault with such a dictator or nation. When another nation decides to enter a war to defend itself from such a potential threat, it undoubtedly has the right to defend itself, but at exactly what point that occurs is never an easy decision for any leader or group of leaders to make.

I do believe that a nation such as ours does have an obligation to defend others who may not be able to defend themselves, just as individuals have an obligation to defend the defenseless. I further believe that this nation has become more complacent about the freedom of other people in the world. Beyond those beliefs the issues involving each war we have been engaged in are probably not as known to me as they would need to be in order to make a broad judgment on the specific morality of each war.

When addressing the unalienable rights as set forth in the Declaration of Independence, I have most frequently addressed the rights of life and liberty and have rarely addressed the unalienable right to the pursuit of happiness. Nevertheless I believe one of the major functions of government beyond the need to protect the life and liberty of its citizens is to create an environment through the laws it creates that permits each and every citizen the right to follow their individual pursuit of happiness. That best occurs when government is least intrusive in the life of its citizens. It is the government's function to create a level playing field for all of its citizens. Governments have rarely been able to ensure that each citizen will pursue their capabilities to an optimal level. That is the responsibility and accountability of each citizen. Government cannot resolve the success or failure of individuals, but government can and should attempt to create a social environment through its Constitution and laws that assume each individual of a society has an equal opportunity for success and the pursuit of happiness.

One of the major concerns of our nation's society today is the struggle over the value system we as a country should share. In attempting to identify the best "value system" this country can follow I use the words "faith-based morality". They are the best words I have been able to find to describe the moral code of conduct that I believe our forefathers intended for this country. Faith-based morality is a delicate balance between religion-based morality and secular-based morality. The cultural struggle in this country today seems to be the struggle between those latter two moral beliefs. It is my hope and my belief that the resolution to that struggle is a return to the value system that gives credence and acceptance to both the "unalienable rights" our forefathers defined in the Declaration of Independence and the "secular rights" set forth in our Constitution. "Flawed Justice" occurs when members of our judicial system and others in government do not recognize the need to observe both the faith-based and secular sets of rights. Without that recognition, the cultural struggle over the appropriate value system will be ongoing.

CHAPTER 6---THE TREATMENT OF NATIVE AMERICANS

While doing some research for this chapter of the book, it seemed that I could write many good things about this country's treatment of Native Americans. Not all the early or even current relationships with the Native Americans were uniformly unjust and many benefited them. However in this book, my chore is to deal with flawed justice.

Conflicts between Native Americans and the early settlers of this country were inevitable, considering their two entirely different cultures. But, when one considers the current cultural and value clashes among our two major political parties it is somewhat surprising that "the melting pot" of this country worked as well as it did between the European settlers and the Native Americans.

The cultural differences were about as different as two cultures could be. Native Americans were primarily tribal people and the Europeans were not. Europeans were primarily Christians or Jewish people and the Native Americans were not. The physical features of the two races were considerably different. The types of dwellings each called home were different. Land ownership was very structured with the Europeans but was not with the Native Americans. Most Native Americans lived in a tribal community setting whereas the European immigrants living in a family setting. The Europeans who came to this country were truly confronted with a race that was very different to anything they had previously confronted or were even aware of. The same was true of the Native Americans.

As noted earlier, one could find many good things to say about the relationship of the two races but the treatment of Native Americans by the new settlers of this land was often harsh. The reverse was also sometimes true. It is difficult to point to any one or two cases by our judicial system that could be called severely flawed justice. The injustice to Native Americans was done by a broader group in government and by society generally.

In looking at the injustices to Native Americans, one must remember this was the land that once be-

longed entirely to them. Granted it was owned or set-
tled in tribal fashion but nevertheless it was their land.
The number of Native Americans that lived here at
the time Columbus discovered this continent is not
precisely known but most estimates put the number in
the millions.

A substantial number of Native Americans, belonging to the tribes along the eastern seaboard, were sub-
jected to slavery during the seventeenth and eighteenth
centuries. For a variety of reasons the ratio of Native
American slaves to African American slaves gradually
diminished. One of the reasons was that the settlers
from Europe brought diseases to this country, which
decimated the Native American population. It was also
easier for the Native American slave to escape and rejoin
his or her tribal community.

The slavery of Native Americans further indicated
that many of the early settlers did not consider them as
equal in terms of humanity. The words in the Declaration of Independence, which assumed it to be a self-
evident truth that all people are created equal, did not
seem to extend to African or Native Americans. Even
after this nation was formed it continued to treat the
Native Americans as less than equal and would not treat
many of them as citizens for many years.

In 1830, Congress passed the Indian Removal Act.
The greed for land that belonged to Native American
tribes was a major motivating factor in passage of the

Act. After considerable debate, the bill was passed and then signed by President Andrew Jackson.

The law resulted in five major tribes located in Florida, Georgia and other southeastern states giving up their land in those areas and relocating to the area that was later to become the state of Oklahoma. At that time the region of Oklahoma was sparsely populated and thought to be of little value.

During the early 1800's, tens of thousands of Native Americans died on the trek from the southeast, across the Mississippi and into Oklahoma. The trail, which the Native Americans traveled, became known as "The Trail of Tears". That injustice would not end with their forced removal to the area of Oklahoma. In the early 20th century, the Native Americans who populated that region would again be forced to move onto reservations.

Throughout the early and mid-nineteenth century the federal government's policy was to move the Native Americans to the west and minimize their contacts with the settlers. Such contacts too often resulted in conflicts between the two. But as settlers kept moving West they continued to move on to the lands that had been occupied by the Native Americans of those regions, including the Sioux, Apache, Nez Perce, Utes and others. Conflicts involving substantial loss of life were waged between the tribes and the US Army. The Sioux at the Little Big Horn River annihilated General Custer and his men and later hundreds of Sioux were killed at Wounded Knee, South Dakota. Many similar battles took place throughout that region of the country.

Beyond the conflicts, other actions led to destroying the way of life for the Native Americans. Buffalo herds on the plains were almost wiped out by excessive hunting. Buffalo had provided food and hides for the Native Americans of that region. The gold rush in the Black Hills of Dakota also impinged on the hunting grounds of the Native Americans of that region. It was not only the government, but also the Army and settlers who made life miserable for the Native Americans.

It was probably inevitable that as more and more settlers moved to the West, efforts would be made to assimilate the Native Americans into the culture of the European immigrants who were becoming more and more numerous in this new country.

In 1887, the General Allotment Act (Dawes Act) was passed by Congress to grant landholdings to individual Native Americans in order to replace tribal holdings. The purpose of the Act was to absorb Native Americans into the larger national society. Even if the Act was well intended, the end result was to put more of the tribal lands into the hands of settlers. The Act also caused a further breakdown in the tribal community culture of Native Americans, regardless of their wishes. It may be that the Act hastened the assimilation of the two cultures but it was a one way street and that street was away from the culture the Native Americans had followed for hundreds of years. It caused a permanent disruption to many Native American mores.

In 1924 the Indian Citizenship Act was passed. By 1924 it was estimated that about two-thirds of Native Americans had gained their citizenship. Some gained it via marriage, some through various treaties that provided citizenship; some achieved it through the Dawes Act and some through other means. In World War I many Native Americans served their country in the military and this gave impetus to the 1924 Act. Numerous Native Americans still lived the communal style of life with their tribes and had not previously been granted citizenship. The Act finally granted the citizenship to many Americans whose ancestors lived on these lands long before the "white man" arrived. The Act also ended the attempt to force the Native Americans to change all their cultural traits inasmuch as it permitted citizenship for those living the tribal style of life, which the Dawes Act did not permit.

In this chapter, and in the previous two chapters we have examined some of the most serious violations of justice committed against large groups of citizens or potential citizens of this country. I will leave it to our Creator to determine if slavery, abortion, or the treatment of Native Americans ranked as the greatest injustice. Some, in our government have in the past ignored faith-based morality and some still do. Too often judges and politicians have found it politically correct to ignore faith-based morality. Political correctness is not entirely new to this country. Adjudication and enforcement of civil law, without taking faith-based morality into consideration, has been and continues to be dangerous and unjust to many in our society.

In each of the three injustices noted above, some branch of government ignored the self-evident truths contained in our Declaration of Independence. In the case of slavery the unalienable rights to liberty and the pursuit of happiness were ignored. In the case of Native Americans, the unalienable rights to liberty and the pursuit of happiness were ignored. In the case of abortions the unalienable rights to life, liberty and the pursuit of happiness were and still are being ignored.

I know that many legal scholars will say that the Declaration of Independence is not a part of the Constitution and should be ignored when interpreting justice as intended by our Constitution and our laws. My response is that our forefathers made it abundantly clear in the Declaration of Independence that all people are created equal and that they are endowed by their Creator with the unalienable rights of life, liberty and the pursuit of happiness. They not only made that abundantly clear but also said that they were self-evident. Those rights were so clear and self-evident to our forefathers that they became enough of a reason to create a new nation. Those rights should not only be recognized, but justice is often lacking when they are not considered. Unalienable rights must always be a higher priority than government granted rights. The latter rights created by government often change but the unalienable rights never change.

When our Constitution and laws are adjudicated in the secular vacuum that ignores faith-based morality, injustice occurs. Secular-based morality alone is simply inadequate to recognize the faith beliefs our forefathers subscribed to when declaring freedom. The Monument to our Forefathers also recognized the need for faith. I want to make it abundantly clear that when I use the word faith, it has a different meaning than the word religion used in the First Amendment. Faith is a necessity in the administration of justice and some specific religious beliefs are not. Adherence to the words in the Declaration would not have permitted the injustices of slavery, the inhumane treatment of Native Americans and would not permit the denial of life to the unborn. Secular judgments without faith-based morality need not lead to diabolical reasoning and diabolical results but it may and it has.

CHAPTER 7---THE PLIGHT OF JAPANESE AMERICANS DURING WW II

World War II had innumerable incidents of tragedies. The atrocities committed against the Jewish people by the Nazi regime are well documented. Everyone who has read Elie Wiesel's *NIGHT* cannot be left without deep feelings of sympathy and compassion for the death of millions of Jewish people, whose only crime was that they belonged to a race that Hitler and his group of fellow Nazis wished to exterminate.

Millions of people in Europe and Asia were also caught up in a war that left them homeless and without what many of us today would consider the bare necessities of daily life. Many lost their homes and many had to struggle to maintain life. The Nazi army entrapped the people of St. Petersburg, Russia for a long period and many did not survive.

In the Far East the Japanese inflicted inhumane treatment on the people of China and the Philippines. Their regime, which was so intent on domination in that region of the world, was treated more humanely by this country after the war than they treated many of the people that were conquered by the armed forces of their country.

However, in this nation the treatment of German-Americans and Italian-Americans was different than the treatment of Japanese-Americans. One can only conclude that some of the reasons were racial. That racism began in the 19th century and continued up to the attack on Pearl Harbor. Their "guilt" far too often was their heritage. Too many Japanese Americans were treated harshly by their fellow Americans, and too many were also treated inhumanely by their government.

Pearl Harbor was attacked on December 7, 1941 and World War II began. At that time, more than 100,000 people of Japanese origin or descent lived on the West Coast. But even prior to Pearl Harbor, the actions of the Japanese armed forces in the Far East aggravated what was already a bad racial situation aimed at not only the Japanese but also other people of Oriental descent. Pearl Harbor brought considerable grief to the Japanese Americans.

Two months after Pearl Harbor was attacked President Roosevelt at the urging of West Coast political leaders issued Executive Order 9066. The issuance of this order was not one of President Roosevelt's finer moments. The second paragraph of that order follows:

Now, therefore by virtue of the authority vested in me as President of the United States, and Commander in Chief of the Army and Navy, I hereby authorize and direct the Secretary of War, and the Military Commanders whom he may from time to time designate to prescribe places and of such extent as he or the appropriate Military Commander may determine, from which any or all persons may be excluded, and which in respect to which, the right of any person to enter, remain in, or leave shall be subject to whatever restriction the Secretary of War or the appropriate Military Commander may impose in his discretion. The Secretary of War is hereby authorized to provide for residents of any such area who are excluded therefrom, such transportation, food, shelter, and other accommodations as may be necessary, in the judgment of the Secretary of War or the said Military Commander and until other arrangements are made, to accomplish the purpose of this order. The designation of military areas in any region or locality shall supersede designation of prohibited and restricted areas by the Attorney General under the Proclamation of December 7 and 8, 1941, and shall supersede the responsibility and authority of the Attorney General under the said Proclamation in respect of such prohibited and restricted areas.

A casual reading of the above does not seem too onerous, but the implementation of the Order would prove to be extremely onerous to the Japanese Americans residing on the West Coast. More than half of those Japanese Americans would end up in relocation centers, which were often located in isolated areas.

Those who were relocated were often required to do so without being able to take along household goods and were often deprived of access to their bank accounts. Homes and farmlands were transferred to others. Executive Order 9066 without doubt was aimed at the Japanese Americans.

Once again a group of people were denied the unalienable right to liberty. Wartime made it somewhat understandable but too often in this country we have found excuses to circumvent the unalienable right to liberty when political, and in these cases military, expediency dictated such questionable action.

The Supreme Court's history with the African Americans was not substantially improved with its actions against Japanese Americans and we will examine several of the cases involving the internment of Japanese Americans during World War II. Much of this information was obtained from Jay M Brown's paper written for the Yale-New Haven's Teachers Institute and from the opinions rendered in the cases.

The case we will analyze at some length is that of Fred Toyosaburo Korematsu versus the United States. Korematsu was a native born Japanese American, whose parents were born in Japan. Korematsu was a citizen of the state of California. Korematsu was not guilty of any crime other than the refusal to comply with Executive Order 9066. He refused to be evacuated and detained and for that alone he was charged.

The case reached the Supreme Court and on December 18, 1944, by a 6 to 3 opinion, the Court affirmed the right of the military to relocate Japanese American citizens pursuant to Executive Order 9066. Once again the Court was confronted with the question of whether it was constitutional under the 5th Amendment to deprive a "person" of life, liberty or property without due process.

The following are the pertinent portions of the majority's opinion delivered by Justice Black:

We uphold the exclusion order as of the time it was made and when the petitioner violated it...In doing so, we are mindful of the hardships imposed by it upon a large group of American citizens...But hardships are part of war, and war is an aggregation of hardships. All citizens alike, both in and out of uniform, feel the impact of war in greater or lesser measure. Citizenship has its responsibilities as well as its privileges, and in time of war the burden is always heavier. Compulsory exclusion of large groups of citizens from their homes, except under circumstances of direct emergency and peril, is inconsistent with our basic governmental institutions. But when under conditions of modern warfare our shores are threatened by hostile forces, the power to protect must be commensurate with the threatened danger...

It is said that we are dealing here with the case of imprisonment of a citizen in a concentration camp solely because his ancestry, without evidence or inquiry concerning his loyalty and good disposition towards the United States. Our task would be simple, our duty clear, were this a case involving the imprisonment of a loyal citizen in a concentration camp because of racial prejudice. Regardless of the true nature of the assembly and relocations centers---and we deem it unjustifiable to call them concentration camps with all the ugly connotations that term implies...we are dealing with an exclusion order. To cast this case into outlines of racial prejudice, without reference to the real military dangers which were presented, merely confuses the issue.

<u>Korematsu was not excluded from the Military Area because of hostility to him or his race. He was excluded because we are at war with the Japanese-Empire, because the properly constituted military authorities feared an invasion of our West Coast and felt constrained to take proper security measures, because they decided that the military urgency of the situation demanded that all citizens of Japanese ancestry be segregated from the West Coast temporarily, and finally, because Congress, reposing its confidence in this time of war in our military leaders---as inevitably it must---determined that they should have the power to do just this.</u>

There was evidence of disloyalty on the part of some, the military authorities considered that the need for action was great, and time was short. We cannot---by availing ourselves of the calm perspective of hindsight---now say that at the time these actions were unjustified.

The above penultimate paragraph is underlined because it was at the heart of the case. Was it true that Korematsu was not excluded from the Military Area because of hostility to him or his race? As noted earlier more than half of the Japanese Americans living on the West Coast were interred. That was not the case with German Americans or Italian Americans and it was Germany and Italy, who were our enemies in Europe. Was the threat different on the West Coast than on the East Coast? There is no answer that can directly indict the decision of the Court but there is no doubt that the Japanese Americans paid a heavy price based on the assumption they were a special threat during that war. There is also no doubt that the war denied them the unalienable right to liberty and the pursuit of happiness.

The Korematsu case was not, as noted earlier, decided unanimously. Because the issue of race was viewed so differently by the minority let us examine some of the dissenting words of Justice Murphy:

The exclusion of "all persons of Japanese, both alien and non-alien," from the Pacific Coast area on a plea of military necessity in the absence of martial law ought not to be approved...

That this forced exclusion was the result in good measure of this erroneous assumption of racial guilt rather than bona fide military necessity is evidenced by the Commanding General's final report on the evacuation from the Pacific Coast area. In it he refers to all individuals of Japanese-descents as "subversive," as belonging to " an enemy race"

<u>*whose "racial strains are undiluted," and as constituting*</u>
<u>*"over 112,000 potential enemies…at large today," along the*</u>
<u>*Pacific Coast. In support of this blanket condemnation of all*</u>
<u>*persons of Japanese descent, however, no reliable evidence is*</u>
<u>*cited…*</u>(underlined for emphasis)

No one denies, of course, that there were some disloyal persons of Japanese descent on the Pacific Coast who did all in their power to aid their ancestral land. Similar disloyal activities have been engaged in by many persons of German, Italian and even more pioneer stock in our country. But to infer that examples of individual disloyalty prove group dis-loyalty and justify discriminatory action against the entire group is to deny that under our system of law individual guilt is the sole basis for deprivation of rights…

*I dissent, therefore, from this legalization of racism. Racial discrimination in any form and in any degree has no justifiable part whatever in our democratic way of life. It is unattractive in any setting but it is utterly revolting among a free people who have embraced the principles set forth in the Constitution of the United States. All residents of this nation are kin in some way by blood or culture to a foreign land. Yet they are primarily and necessarily a part of the new and distinct civilization of the United States. They must accordingly be treated at all times as the heirs of the American experiment and as entitled to all the rights and freedo*ms guaranteed by the Constitution.

So, who was right? The future often sheds more light on the past. Most people who would look at the same facts, sixty-plus years after the case was heard would probably side with Justice Murphy, who at that time was one of the minority of three judges. This much can be said. The interment of many, if not most, who were innocent victims, was a violation of their unalienable right to liberty, set forth in the Declaration of Independence. It was also a violation of their 5th Amendment right of due process.

The Supreme Court decided two additional cases involving Japanese Americans, who refused to be relocated. In 1943, Kiyoshi Hirabayashi, who was a student at the University of Washington and Minoru Yasui, an attorney from Portland, Oregon both challenged the evacuation orders. In both cases the Court sided with the government for many of the same reasons it did in the Korematsu case.

In each of the cases the Court essentially decided that the government had the power during wartime to insure the security of the country over the right of individuals to be granted the right of liberty provided in the 5th Amendment. That sounds reasonable on the surface, but when the unalienable right of liberty is denied, the greatest of care must be taken to insure the rights of innocent people.

In this and my other books I have often blamed the courts for upholding the civil rights of individuals at the expense of the general welfare of the entire population. In the case of Japanese Americans interred during World War II the opposite problem occurred.

Far too many innocent people were interred who were not threats to the general welfare of the country.

Once the Court was able to establish that the individuals who challenged the sweeping broad relocations did not present a threat, the Court should have sided with the individual's rights contained in the 5th Amendment. In that manner the court would have also upheld the national morality and a higher level of justice intended by our founding fathers and proclaimed that it was a self-evident truth that there was an unalienable right to liberty.

CHAPTER 8 --- INJUSTICES TO OUR CHILDREN

In our society today and in the history of our nation, children are and have been treated unjustly without the opportunity for any recourse. They are not permitted to vote. In this example of flawed justice, the courts again share much of the blame but they are not the only ones who inflict injustice upon our children. Such injustice is also the fault of other branches of government as well as all of society, especially parents.

In this book and the previous books written by me, I have deplored this nation's aiding and abetting in the terrible crime of abortion. There is little more to add than what I have already written on the subject of abortion. Abortion is an abhorrent practice when not endorsed by government. When government endorses it as it did in Roe vs. Wade, it brings shame to an entire nation. Abortion provides an excuse to terrorists to denounce this nation.

Abortion is an injustice to unborn human beings but injustices have also been extended to those already born. Considering that our children are the ones who will some day grow up and be the doctors, lawyers, ministers, nurses and business leaders of the future, parents and government should be in unison in providing the best possible environment for those youngsters.

Until the urbanization of this country it was understandable that children assisted in the chores and labors of households that were largely agrarian. My own childhood included many of those chores with which most of the current citizens of this nation are no longer familiar. It included chopping and bringing in the wood for the wood-burning stoves, rounding up the cattle for milking, assisting in the hay field, as well as gardening and many of the other chores of those in rural America in the late 1930's and 1940's. Those chores in no way were an injustice to those of us who experienced doing them. They provided a work discipline to our lives that would stand us in good stead as we became older.

But the industrialization of this nation brought types of work that were not appropriate for children but which children did experience. As this nation became industrialized the demand for labor grew and from the mid-and-late 19th century until the early 20th century that expansion too often included children. In the late 19th century and early 20th century groups were formed to protest this labor abuse of children. Among the concerns of these groups was that factory work often deprived children of an education.

In 1904 the National Child Labor Committee was formed and by 1912 a Children's Bureau was established by the government as a federal information clearing-house. A year later this Bureau became a part of the Department of Labor. The government had put into place the vehicle that would help correct the abuse of child labor.

In 1916, Congress passed the Keating-Owens Act, which was signed into law by President Wood-row Wilson. It was the first law that regulated child labor. It established standards of permissible working hours and minimum ages for certain types of labor. It also included a restriction of the interstate shipment of goods produced by child labor. Because of the latter provision in the law, the Supreme Court in the Hammer vs. Dagenhart case found the Keating-Owens Act unconstitutional because of the restriction on interstate commerce.

Once again the Supreme Court found an entire law passed by Congress unconstitutional due to one provision of the law although other provisions of the law, which regulated child labor enhanced the general welfare of the country. It would again have been a better system if the Supreme Court did not have the power to strike down an entire law, much of which was good law. It would also have been better to refer back to Congress that portion of the law that was a problem regarding interstate commerce and have the law amended as necessary by Congress to correct the concerns of the Supreme Court.

But the abuse of child labor was diminishing and under the early reforms passed during the early presidential years of Franklin D Roosevelt the remaining issues permitting abusive child labor were eliminated.

But the abuse of our children did not end with child labor laws. We continue to have sexual abuse of our children without the adequate punishment of such crimes and we have the neglect of too many children under new moral standards being adopted by this nation.

In recent years we have seen the sexual and physical abuse of children accompanied by very minor punishment from judges. As this book is being written efforts are underway by states to pass mandatory punishment under legislation referred to as "Jessica's Law".

This law was named after a young Florida girl, Jessica Lunsford, who was brutally raped and murdered by a previously convicted sex offender.

The key provisions of Jessica's Law mandate a minimum sentence of 25 years in prison for adults convicted of lewd or lascivious molestation of a victim under the age of 12. The law also requires lifetime monitoring of adults who are responsible for such crimes.

It would seem that all state legislators would rush to the forefront of such legislation, but that is not the case. It would also seem that the legal profession would uniformly endorse such legislation, but that too is not the case. And it would also seem that judges would be happy to have such sentencing guidelines to help protect our children, but that too is not always the case.

One of the major reasons that Jessica's Law is being passed in many states is the work done by Bill O'Reilly of the Fox News Channel. He is a tireless and outspoken advocate of the passage of Jessica's Law in all states. His efforts are producing results.

The injustices to children may also be coming from a more subtle form of abuse and neglect. In my earlier book "Redefining Morality - A Threat to our Nation" I addressed the dangers to our nation of redefining the morality intended by our founding fathers. I did not address what the effects of redefining that morality may have on our children but will do so for the remainder of this chapter.

In recent years the number of children that no longer come from nuclear family homes is increasing. We cannot state with certainty what the moral effect of that will be on children but we can certainly note the issues.

Throughout the entire history of the universe, the most widely accepted makeup of a family has been that of the biological father, biological mother and their biological children. There have been other periods of time such as we are currently experiencing, when the nuclear family has not been given the status it deserves in society. That was the case when the Roman Empire existed. That empire too lost its moral compass and decayed from within.

What place in society does the nuclear family deserve? If we fully understand the moral and human role that the family plays, we should value it a great deal. We should especially try to understand the impact of the nuclear family on children.

At the present time the United States has more children living outside a nuclear family than at any time in its history. It makes a child's life more difficult. When a single mother has to be away from the home to provide a livelihood for herself and her children and no father is present in the home, that child suffers. The lack of parental guidance is a problem especially in a society where morality is absent in government and schools. If not from parents, where can children get such moral guidance?

Those who fight for greater and too often immoral freedom of speech and expression on TV, movies, and essentially all forms of media, use the argument that it is up to the parents to provide moral guidance and to monitor their children's activities insofar as watching what children see on TV or in the movies. But they don't answer the question of how that is possible when parents play a smaller role in the life of a child.

The preamble of our Constitution states that the Constitution is there to provide for the general welfare of all citizens. Nowhere in the Constitution does it state how that is to be achieved for children. What do we need to provide for the general welfare of our children?

With more women in the workplace, it follows that women have less time to devote to parenting. The sociological impact of that situation has yet to be determined. The father's influence on children too has diminished. A smaller percentage of biological fathers are now a part of children's lives due to fewer being married and due to a higher number of divorces. Therefore, many children no longer receive the discipline and teaching that historically came from the biological father. That puts a greater need on the teachings and directions of the biological mother and because she must often be in the workplace, the parenting is simply absent in too many lives of today's children. Thus the children of today too often miss receiving moral guidance from parents, which once was an assumed guidance for all children.

Too many in our society have accepted the diminished role of traditional marriage between a man and woman. Too many in our society have accepted the increased percentage of divorces. Too many in our society have accepted that children can get along without the need for more parental guidance. Too many in our society accept that morality is not to be a part of the classroom. How do we then expect our children to understand the benefits of morality? How do we expect our children to understand the words of George Washington that reason and experience forbid us to believe that a national morality can exist in the absence of religious principles? How can we expect children to even believe that such a morality is important to a society, when there is no one around to teach him or her of that importance?

Is a child's life enhanced because constraints on sexual activities are no longer a part of our traditional moral values? Is a child's life enhanced because pornographic material is available on TV, magazine racks, movies and other media? Is a child's life enhanced from the sports and other activities that now dwell on greater and greater violence? Is a child's life enhanced from exposure to drugs at any early age? Is a child's life enhanced from the constantly diminished status of faith and the symbols of faith? Does society help its children when it cannot distinguish faith from religious and therefore frequently puts a ban on the symbols of both? Do judges help children when they let child predators pay very small penalties for their offenses? Even if both parents were available, can they monitor the 24-hour activities of children in a society that has very few moral boundaries for them?

In an amoral society, raising children to become good citizens of a nation is a task that is getting ever-more difficult.

So what is it specifically that our children are really missing? In my view they too frequently lack the moral teaching that George Washington noted when he said that reason and experience forbid us to believe that a national morality can exist in the absence of some religious principles.

Our children are missing the teaching that comes from a strong belief in faith and that it should be a self-evident truth that we are endowed by our Creator (and not by other humans) with certain unalienable rights and that such rights include life, liberty and the pursuit of happiness. It requires faith in a Creator to believe what our founding fathers understood makes for a better nation. People of all religions are better people when they possess and demonstrate a faith in a good and kind Creator. In a society that is becoming more secular, the secularists set aside the belief that our most precious rights are bestowed by our Creator. Our children need to understand those self-evident truths. Faith in that belief noted in our Declaration of Independence is the foundation necessary to make better future citizens. Faith IS the foundation of our national faith-based morality.

Too many of our children are also missing the values of love and consideration that comes from being part of a nuclear family. It is difficult to bestow those values when parents are not the ones instilling and demonstrating such values. Love of family, friends and neighbors IS also a necessary ingredient of a national faith based morality.

Too many children also do not understand the benefits of hard work and sacrifice. Far too many are embracing the immediate gratification in a country that is placing ever-greater value on materialistic resources and desires. In that environment it is difficult to sustain our national faith-based morality.

Without teaching our children the basic goodness of faith in our Creator, love of family, friends and neighbors, and the importance of hard work and sacrifice, we fail our children.

It is a responsibility of parents. It is a responsibility of educators. It is a responsibility of religions. It is also the responsibility of government to create an environment in which our national faith-based morality can and should be passed on to our children

It should come as no surprise that opinion polls indicate our governmental bodies are no longer held in high regard. Too many in government forget that virtue and morality are the springboards of popular government. The words of our Constitution and laws can be twisted and interpreted from an amoral and totally secular perspective. When that is done government begins forgetting the SELF-EVIDENT TRUTHS our founding fathers proclaimed when this nation was created. They also overlook the words GENERAL WELFARE from the preamble to our Constitution. It is especially the members of our judicial system who forget that justice is diminished when morality is diminished and that both are diminished when faith is absent. When any members of government today believe they have a greater insight than our founding fathers had as to what is necessary to make a great nation they are most likely wrong.

It is especially our future generations that suffer most from a government and a society that has lost its moral compass too frequently.

CHAPTER 9---JUSTICE REQUIRES MORALITY

In this book, injustices to large groups of our population have been noted. Injustices have been committed against African Americans, Native Americans, Japanese Americans, our children and unborn human beings. In all cases the injustices have occurred because the self-evident truths for which our forefathers founded this nation were ignored. In all the history of the universe, no better words have been used for nations to be formed. When our forefathers' view of a national morality has been observed, justice for all has been maintained to the best extent possible. When ignored, the results have been dismal as noted in the chapters of this book.

We cannot have justice, especially legal justice, when we ignore the self-evident truth that all human beings in this nation have the unalienable right to life, liberty and the pursuit of happiness. No one in government or in any other position has the moral and justifiable right to remove an unalienable right for other human beings. They are bestowed to each of us by our Creator. They are unalienable. It is worth repeating that the greatest travesties of justice in the history of this nation occurred when our government and especially our justice system ignored those unalienable rights.

Virtue and morality are ignored when our unalienable rights are ignored. As President Washington noted, virtue and morality are the necessary spring to maintain a popular government. It is no accident that the popularity of our government has waned in recent history.

President Washington also stated that experience and reason should make us understand that our national faith-based morality on which this nation was founded must be based on some religious principles in order to prevail. Considering the words of the First Amendment it may be that faith would have been a better choice of words than "religious principles" but he apparently drew no distinctions between religious principles and faith.

In declaring our independence, our founding fathers justified that independence on the belief that some self-evident truths exist, which are based on the most simple of all faith beliefs; the belief in a Creator who endows human beings with unalienable rights. They obviously saw no contradiction in that belief and in the words of the First Amendment. After all, many of the forefathers were involved with both the Declaration of Independence and the First Amendment. .

That faith belief is the basis of what President Washington referred to as our national morality. That belief combined with a sincere concern for and promotion of the general welfare for all plus the civil rights of each individual form the foundation of our justice system and our national morality.

As noted in Chapter 1, justice and morality are interdependent and both require faith. Yes, "reason and experience" forbid us to think otherwise. No government in the history of the universe has continued to prevail in the absence of the "national morality" established by our founding fathers. The government they founded was and is a unique effort to establish a government on the belief that "religious principles" or what I refer to as a faith-based morality were a necessity to maintain "popular government".

As stated by many "eternal vigilance is the price of freedom". Eternal vigilance is also the price of maintaining our national faith-based morality.

In the past fifty years we have begun departing from the national faith-based morality intended by our founding fathers. We have begun relying more and more on a solely secular morality in the establishment of laws and adjudication of justice. Individual rights are being upheld even when they are to the detriment of the general welfare. The greatest injustice of current history is the abortion of more than 45 million human beings since 1973. It is a travesty that the Supreme Court of this nation gave its approval to the termination of the unalienable right to life. It is a travesty that only 50 percent of the members of our Congress approve of the unalienable right to life. It is a tragedy that 50 percent of the members of our society believe it is justifiable to permit the right to privacy to be a greater right than the unalienable right to life.

A nation without a proper understanding of justice and morality begins down a slippery path toward a weaker and amoral society. A nation that dismisses the faith of our founding fathers does so at its own peril. When government and a large majority of the population fail to be vigilant in the pursuit of every human being's right to life and liberty, that society may pay the terrible price of trying to maintain justice in the absence of the proper moral code.

We included Chapter 3, "The Maligned First Amendment" in this book because too many in government, especially in our justice system, are unable to any longer distinguish between faith and religion.

One does not need to belong to any religion to have faith that "the self-evident truths" noted by our founding fathers were evident to most people at the beginning of this nation and still should be self-evident to most Americans.

One does not need to belong to any religion to have the faith that the promotion of the general welfare for all human beings including African Americans, Native Americans, Japanese Americans, children and the unborn children via kindness and treating each other as we wish to be treated is an ingredient for a better nation and a better world.

One does not need to belong to any specific religion to have the faith that all individuals on the face of this earth are created equal.

No, one does not need to belong to a specific religion to believe these things. A better world with the proper national morality will exist when a preponderance of a nation's citizens have the faith that our unalienable rights, the general welfare of all, and every individuals rights are the most fundamental of values in the establishment of justice, and especially legal justice. Those rights should extend to our unborn human beings. Hopefully, we have enumerated what happens when we begin depriving people the status of citizenship.

Justice went awry in Nazi Germany, Communist Russia, and dictatorial Iraq when the faith-based ingredients of morality were dismissed and justice also goes awry for African Americans, Native Americans and the aborted unborn when the fundamental requirements of our national morality and national justice are ignored.

When our national faith-based morality is ignored, justice easily becomes FLAWED.

It is not only the government and the justice system within a government that become flawed when the fundamentals of morality are ignored. In the course of history, atrocities have also been committed in the name of religion. The fundamental tenets of most religions are good and should lead the people belonging to such religions to a more moral and purposeful life. But sometimes the leaders and people proclaiming to do things in the name of a religion pervert the good tenets of a religion.

In the world today, fanatical extremists of the Muslim religion are willing to kill themselves and others in the name of their religion. No one could do that who sincerely believes that it is our Creator who endows us with the unalienable right to life.

On the other side of the equation, Muslims and people of other foreign nationalities have a right to view our nation with some dismay.

We too have people who proclaim to be religious, while approving of the death penalty, euthanasia, and abortions. No one could do that who sincerely and truly believes our Creator endows us with the unalienable right to life.

We too have people who believe that the potential, albeit unproven, cure from killing human embryos is acceptable. No one could believe that who sincerely and truly believes that our Creator endows an embryo with the unalienable right to life.

I hasten to add that we should vigorously pursue stem cell research, but should not kill human embryos in that pursuit.

Not all succumb to the tug of secular morality. We can find role models in current times, who possess a wonderful and proper faith-based morality and justice in what they do. Mother Teresa, who labored many years among the poor of India, exhibited in daily life the fundamentals of morality and justice. She truly understood that the life of every individual formed by our Creator was precious and created equal. Few people have gone to greater lengths than she did in order to perpetuate the unalienable right to life, extend human kindness and promote the general welfare. It was her faith as much as her religion that persuaded her to do her extraordinary work among the poorest of the poor.

If we wish to look for role models who had the necessary human ingredients to form an ideal government, we need to look no further than those responsible for establishing the government of this nation. No individual or group of individuals have every ever done a better job in creating a government than did our founding fathers. If those in government today wish to form a more perfect government they only need to emulate our founding fathers. Maybe more importantly, they need to believe what our founding fathers believed was necessary to have a great government.

If those who are members of our judicial system wish to adjudicate in a better manner they only need to study the basic reasons this government was created.

We were a unique model and a JUST nation because our founding fathers believed and proclaimed what they called self-evident truths. We need more believers.

CHAPTER 10---A BETTER SYSTEM

As was noted in the Introduction, justice is defined in many ways. In this book we have reviewed primarily flaws in our legal justice system. It is a valid question to ask if a legal justice system is tied to other forms of justice such as social or economic justice. In my view the answer is yes because all forms of justice depend on morality and both depend on faith. That is the message provided to us by *THE NATIONAL MONUMENT TO THE FOREFATHERS*.

Are such other forms of justice dependent on the government of a country or might they be dependent on others things as well? Government plays a substantial role but so do parental guidance, education, religion, community and other environmental factors. It is my personal belief that our faith, our morality and our sense of justice are gifts from our Creator enhanced by the factors in our life, which I have just noted. That also seems to have been the view of our first President and other founding fathers. Some accept that gift and some do not. It never ceases to amaze me that the acceptance of the gift of faith can vary so greatly, even within family members.

At a recent dinner I attended, the conversation turned to whether socialism or capitalism provided greater justice and values to a society and its citizens. In this nation we have maintained a free enterprise system and it has functioned reasonably well. It has provided many small entrepreneurs with great opportunities. It has also been at times an abusive system. In the 19th century, many of the large corporations and trusts took unfair advantage of the working class. Government was required to step in and establish reforms.

Labor unions also came along, which ensured greater economic justice for workers. One human flaw of our free enterprise system is that owners or management too frequently treat their working force as a commodity.

Socialism is worse because it too frequently leads to dictatorial practices and sometimes dictators and history should certainly teach us that socialism can be very onerous for the working class. Socialism sounds good in theory, but it has a dismal track record.

Reforms and laws have been enacted by our government to ensure or attempt to ensure a fair playing field, which maintains a capitalistic system while protecting the interest of shareholders, employees and customers. If one truly believes that liberty or freedom is an unalienable right granted by our Creator than it follows that the free enterprise system and capitalistic system with appropriate controls remain the best, albeit imperfect, economic system. Nevertheless, the free enterprise system needs the checks and balances of laws and regulations, as does government itself.

In the corporate world of today some corrective measures would provide citizens with a better appreciation of our economic system. The ratio of pay between senior executives, especially the chief executive officer, and workers has grown to an unjustifiable amount. Abuses, such as those which took place at Enron, also bring about reasons to further control corporate management. When management abuses the economic free enterprise system, it invites greater governmental oversight and restrictive legislation. Abuses in all aspects of a free society invite constraints and thus freedom itself is eroded.

It is said that the best test of social justice is the manner in which a society treats the most vulnerable and defenseless human beings within the society. No better words exist for government and citizens than those words of the Golden Rule, "Do unto others as you would have them do unto you". These words are among the fundamental requirements of social and legal justice. Adherence to those words would also not have permitted the existence of slavery and the other injustices noted in this book.

The major continuing legal, moral and social injustice in this country is the ongoing number of abortions of our unborn children that is permitted by our justice system. It is estimated that more than 45 million unborn human beings have been aborted since the Supreme Court decisions of Roe vs. Wade and Doe vs. Bolton made abortions legally permissible in this country. It is a tragedy. It is barbaric. It is as flawed as justice can possibly be. It has deprived more than 45 million human beings of the unalienable right to life. The aforementioned Supreme Court decisions permit society to kill the most vulnerable and defenseless of all human beings and thereby this nation flunks that significant test of social justice for all.

Human failures also require checks and balances. Because we are flawed human beings, we must have laws against murder, cheating, stealing, etc. Greed and power must find restraint through the civil laws of government and government itself must be restrained via a system of check and balances imposed by self-evident truths and by a Constitution. Our founding fathers blueprint for such checks and balances were and still are the best example of how to provide the optimal level of opportunity and justice for all citizens.

When we as a nation deviate from the model given us by our founding fathers we deviate from the foundation of what truly made us a great government. It was and is a great country because it is a good country. It will only remain a great country if it remains a good country. It will only remain a good country if we adhere to the national morality perceived for this country by our founding fathers.

As this nation has grown so also have the number of laws governing it. Caution should be exercised when new laws are passed. Excessive legislation is a constraint on liberty and we should never forget that liberty too is an unalienable right. Nevertheless, when our rights as free people are abused we must turn to our government for corrective action. Freedom cries for a minimum of legislation but freedom needs vigilance and vigilance is provided through a minimum but necessary amount of laws and regulations. The balance between the amount of freedom we enjoy and the number of laws required is a delicate but necessary function of government.

When the laws are appropriate and our rights are abused we must look to our judicial system of government to correct those abuses. It is of the utmost importance that the members of our judicial system understand the fundamentals of justice noted in the first chapter of this book. It is not enough to merely understand the law. We have attempted to note the injustices to large groups in this country when the judicial system has failed and why those failures occurred.

Judges and jurists are human and humans err. I take to heart the cautions this book has given to others in changing what our founding fathers intended and I would change very little in what our founding fathers provided as guidance for the judicial system.

One significant change is required to our judicial system. We should not permit the Supreme Court or lower courts to overturn the legislation enacted by Congress, as we noted in Chapter 1. Permitting the Supreme Court to do so gives them dictatorial power and that power has and can continue to diminish the system of checks and balances intended by our founding fathers.

Maybe of greater importance for the good of our society is that all citizens of this country understand, promote, believe in and adhere to the national faith-based morality mentioned by our first President in his farewell address on September 17, 1796. History, reason and experience demand it of a nation that wishes to maintain its status as one of the greatest nations ever conceived by humans.

ABOUT THE AUTHOR

George E Pfautsch spent most of his working life as a financial executive for a major forests products and paper company. His final years at Potlatch Corporation were spent as the Senior Vice-President of Finance and Chief Financial Officer. Following his retirement he began writing and speaking on the national morality he believes was intended for this nation by the founding fathers of our country. In his first book, REDEFINING MORALITY-A THREAT TO OUR NATION, he examined the new secular standards of this country that are undermining the principles our founding father intended as a cornerstone to our Constitution and laws. In his second book, TIMES OF GREATNESS – MORALITY MATTERS, Pfautsch reviewed the history of our nation and the role that the national faith-based morality intended by our founding fathers. In his second book, TIMES OF GREATNESS-MORALITY MATTERS, Pfautsch reviewed the history of our nation and the role that the national faith-based morality intended by our founding fathers <u>played in the greatest periods of our nation</u>.

www.ingramcontent.com/pod-product-compliance
Lightning Source LLC
Chambersburg PA
CBHW020313290526
45784CB00003B/1493